MISPLACED
RIGHTEOUSNESS

Why God takes NO PART *in Religion*

A U S T I N D E B O U R G

ISBN: 1491289910
ISBN 13: 9781491289914
Library of Congress Control Number: 2013914636
CreateSpace Independent Publishing Platform
North Charleston, South Carolina

A Little Book with a Big Message

Truth is essential for the preservation of godliness and for the benefit of all, irrespective of opposition in whatever form it may present itself. Those committed to the dispensing of truth cannot afford to succumb to the temptation of silence. The Spirit of Truth needs to be allowed back into the lives of believers of Jesus Christ and into the house of God.

The truth that made Christianity the dynamic voice and a demonstration for God on the earth must be recovered now!

God is absolute, specific, and permanent. God and His Word are not subject to alteration, exclusion, addition, or private or personal interpretation. God's Word harmonizes with itself in content, and when used in proper context.

Religion is freestyled and therefore accommodates multiplicity, allowing everyone and anyone to determine their own belief, philosophy, structure, and expression. Specific religious systems can be distinguished by the conduct of rituals and forms of worship, and often involve a code of ethics and philosophy.

There is no absolute in religion!

God's Word and religion do not harmonize. They are opposites like day and night are opposites. God is God, and religion is religion! God did not ordain religion!

Religion does not determine how man gets to heaven.

Contents

Introduction

Misplaced Righteousness is a little book with a big, sensitive message—Righteousness. It is sensitive because righteousness has been interpreted in countless ways by countless Christian and religious bodies, each determining and practicing their interpretation of righteousness, and each purporting that their interpretation is the true and correct one. It is misplaced thinking for one to believe that righteousness could have so many different and varied interpretations, as exists today, and that God accepts them all. To continue along this path would only lead to further fragmentation of thought and spiritual damage to persons who have a desire to properly align themselves with God.

Misplaced Righteousness seeks to direct the reader to the meaning of righteousness from God's perspective, and examines how He expects us to practice it. Certainly, God's righteousness is not man's righteousness, as this book will reveal. It will also clearly point out where and how these two differ.

Additionally, this book addresses the deviations, distortions, and misrepresentations of other biblical truths, which are today accepted as truth.

God is the source and the author of the doctrine of righteousness, and, therefore, He must be the one to give us the meaning and interpretation of this, and of all His doctrines, principles, and truths. God would not leave it up to the limited minds of individuals to put their own meaning and interpretation to His Word, His principles, and His truths. Should He do so, He would leave Himself vulnerable to being misunderstood, and would also create avenues to be discredited as the Supreme, All-Mighty, All-Wise God. God has never given over this right to anyone.

My goal is that, through this book, any misconceptions you may have regarding righteousness would be understood from a biblical perspective so that God's ways would be adopted and passed on to others for the benefit of all. It is indeed God's desire that all may find the right path to His righteousness.

It is my hope that those who have a desire to have the power of the Holy Spirit operating in the Church again, and those Christians who are interested in the restoration and propagation of biblical Christianity, consider the contents of this book. It would help many to recover from the satanic trap into which they have fallen by misinterpreting and compromising God's word.

God is not a loser. He will, one day, restore His truths and have a people who will live by them, and who will again accomplish His purpose on the earth. God Himself said so, as documented in the book of Numbers:

> *But as truly as I live, all the earth shall be filled with the glory of the LORD.*
>
> *—Numbers 14:21*

God's truth will again be heard, and His majesty will be seen and experienced by all.

Chapter 1

Righteousness: A Grossly Distorted Biblical Principle

❧❦

To think that we can become righteous
through anything that we can do, in
ourselves, is erroneous thinking.

❧❦

The doctrine and principles of righteousness, and how to acquire it, have been misunderstood, misinterpreted, and misrepresented for a very long time. This error has opened the door for religious, judgmental, and other deadly spirits to infiltrate the pulpit and then overflow to the congregation.

It is imperative for God's people to have the proper knowledge of God and a right understanding of His Word so that what they believe, teach, preach, and practice as righteousness is indeed what God calls righteousness, and not what misplaced thinking regards as righteousness. Misplaced thinking, with regard to righteousness, is dangerous and destructive. We must recall that God stated:

> *My people are destroyed for lack of knowledge, and because thou hast rejected knowledge, I would also reject thee.*
>
> *—Hosea 4:6*

Misplaced thinking occurs when men arrive at their own private interpretation of God's Word. Note, however, that God's Word is not open to private interpretation. When I speak of righteousness, I am careful not to give my own interpretation, but rather, I allow the Bible to interpret itself using the formula which God has given to us to do so:

> *Whom shall he teach knowledge? and whom shall he make to understand doctrine? them that are weaned from the milk, and drawn from the breasts. [10] For* **precept must be upon precept**, *precept upon precept;* **line upon line,** *line upon line; here a little, and there a little:*
>
> *—Isaiah 28:9–10 (Bold for emphasis)*

God's Word does not contradict itself. God teaches us to search the entire Bible to come into the full understanding of a truth, comparing precept to precept and line to line.

☙❧

The world's systems have changed.
Man's thinking about God has
changed. However, God and His Word
have not changed.

☙❧

In the case of the doctrine of righteousness, the Bible tells us, "There is none righteousness, no, not one" (Romans 3:10), and further states, "we are all as an unclean thing, and all our righteousness are as filthy rags" (Isaiah 64:6). To think therefore, that we can become righteous through anything that we can do, in ourselves, is erroneous thinking. Benevolence and all acts of kindness are good and needful, but when those acts are regarded as righteousness, this is misplaced thinking for God has said that they are "filthy rags" in His sight. Further still, to assume a standard for the judgment of righteousness which emanates from one's private interpretation will result in misplaced righteousness. Righteousness comes from God alone. Simply defined, righteousness is being in right standing with God and He alone determines who qualifies to attain to His imputed righteousness. His decision is based upon one's proven love, faith, and obedience to Him, His Word, and His will. Man must therefore strive to meet God's requirements in order to attain to His righteousness, rather than try to establish his own righteousness which God refers to as "filthy rags." We will further explore this doctrine of righteousness in the chapters of this book.

The world's systems have changed. Man's thinking about God has changed. However, God and His Word have not changed. In spite of how the world views God, His Word, Jesus Christ, and Christianity today, God still expects His people to live by the true knowledge of Himself and His Word. The devil knows that if he could get the people of God to believe and practice error they would destroy themselves. This plan of Satan started with our first parents, Adam and Eve. Satan had distorted God's Word to Eve. Eve accepted it and took that distorted word to Adam. Adam accepted it and this brought about their separation from God and, by extension, ours.

Today, The Church of Jesus Christ has lost the influence which the early Christians had brought to the world. This is as a result of the distortion of God's Word and principles.

One of the young ministers under my leadership, Reverend Jacqueline Martinez, a very prolific preacher of the Word of God, preached a sermon entitled, "The Thief Called Compromise." In it, she identifies how the Church got to where it is today. The devil has certainly used compromise to neutralize the Christians' effectiveness, and the power of the Holy Spirit in the Church and in the world. Compromise is deviation from God's biblical truths to half-truths, or to religion, with its man-made doctrines which are often presented under the guise of truth. Half-truths and religion do not and cannot serve the purposes of God. There are no half-truths in the Word of God. Neither Jesus nor His message is based on half-truths. Jesus is all truth and His message is all truth. If we are to represent Jesus Christ with faithfulness and integrity, we must not engage in the compromising of truth. Any attempt to do so is a betrayal of Jesus Christ who calls and appoints servants to faithfully represent Him to the people.

The Church today is a victim of much misrepresentation and distortion and, as such, has atrophied into an anemic organism, quite different from the Church which we see represented in *The Acts of the Apostles*. Today, misplaced righteousness is accepted as true righteousness.

Chapter 2

God Takes No Part in Religion

❧

God is about relationship—that of a
Father with His children.

❧

Before proceeding any further, let it be known here and now that God did not ordain religion and therefore, God takes no part in religion! God is about relationship—that of a Father with His children. Some have experienced gross disappointment and dis-illusion with religion and, as a result, have distanced themselves from God because they thought that He was in religion. It is essential, therefore, for me to make a clear distinction between God and Religion. This would help to highlight deviations from truth, and distortions of thought. Further still, an aware-ness of this distinction would help to correct and even avoid the confusion that arises through misrepresentation of God's Word.

God is absolute, specific, and permanent. His Word is not subject to alteration, exclusion, addition, or to private or personal interpretation. God's Word, when used in context, harmonizes with itself in content. God's Word does not contradict itself.

Jesus Christ did not establish a religion and call it Christianity.

Religion, on the other hand, is freestyled and therefore accommodates multiplicity, allowing everyone and anyone to determine their own belief, philosophy, structure, and expression. Specific religious systems can be distinguished by the conduct of rituals and forms of worship, and often involve a code of ethics and philosophy.

There is no absolute in religion!

God's Word and religion, therefore, do not harmonize. They are opposites like day and night are opposites. God is God, and religion is religion!

Jesus Christ did not establish a religion and call it Christianity. He established relationship between

Himself and His followers, bringing them into fellowship with God as Father through the experience of a spiritual rebirth and the infilling of His Spirit. This is Biblical Christianity as established by Jesus Christ, and it is all about relationship. It is this relationship that was lost when Adam and Eve sinned against God by their disobedience to His command. God's interaction with Adam and Eve was one of intimacy between Father and children. At no time did God introduce religion into His relationship with Adam and Eve, His first children. He never gave them religious duties and rituals to perform in order to know Him and relate to Him. God's relationship with Adam and Eve involved dialogue and communion with them, and was so personal and intimate that every day God would leave heaven and come to earth to have fellowship with them. The Father so trusted His son, Adam, that He gave him the right to name all the animals He had created. God's ultimate intention and plan for man was and still is a "sonship-relationship" and all that comes with it. Any other thought, idea or belief, on man's part, is contrary to God's Word.

Adam's relationship with God and, by extension, the relationship of all men with God, was severed through his disobedience. Jesus Christ came to restore man to relationship and fellowship with the Father. Again, no religious acts were introduced and no conduct of rituals or philosophies was ever prescribed by Jesus Christ to accomplish this. Religion had no place and no part in that process.

Even the Church which was established by Jesus Christ on His departure comprised a body of believers who would relate to Him and to each other in love. Jesus did not sanction the erection of a building to be named *The Church*. In the course of time, buildings were constructed purely as meeting places for the believers in Christ to congregate, to worship, and to be taught from the scriptures how man should relate to Jesus Christ, to God the Father, and to each other.

> *Moreover if thy brother shall trespass against thee, go and tell him his fault between thee and him alone: if he shall hear thee, thou hast gained thy brother.* ¹⁶*But if he will not hear thee, then take with thee one or two more, that in the mouth of two or three witnesses every word may be established.* ¹⁷*And if he shall neglect to hear them, tell it unto **the church**: but if he neglect to hear **the church**, let him be unto thee as an heathen man and a publican.*
> —Matthew 18:15–17 (Bold for emphasis)

The building never was and still is not *The Church* but the Church is the body of believers which Jesus regards as His very own body, so intimate is the relationship. Again, He was establishing relationship, not the performance of religious acts that would prevent man from having a relationship with God.

God's plan for man has always catered for relationship: firstly, with God Himself and then with each other wherein brotherhood, peace, and goodwill would abound. God's plan alone can restore us to relationship with Him, and not the plan of any other. That plan is clearly seen in His Word. It is therefore vital that we come to know and to rely only on His Word, and to be educated and guided in the way He prescribes.

இ~ி

> If we think wrong, we believe wrong,
> and we act in accordance with our
> wrong thinking and beliefs.

இ~ி

The reality is, however, that we tend to be products of our environment. We often believe what we are taught, whether it be custom, tradition, religion, or the Word of God. Children usually adopt whatever belief their parents pass on to them, and it becomes their faith, whether it is religion, or relationship with God through Jesus Christ. As a general rule, what we think and what we believe form the core of our nature and character. If we think wrong, we believe wrong, and we act in accordance with our wrong thinking and beliefs. Conversely, if we think right, we believe right, and act in accordance with our right thinking and beliefs. Therefore, if we have not been taught what is in the Word of God, and taught it in its proper context, we would not come to know God and His will for our life. We would not come to know that what He desires is relationship.

We cannot deny the influence of our upbringing on what we believe. If the environment in which we live does not convey the truth of God's Word we would automatically be subjected to the consequences of error. Nevertheless, God is always reaching out to us to draw us to Himself.

God has placed within every individual a God-consciousness so that we might desire Him and seek Him through His Word. Note carefully that every individual, when he reaches the age of accountability, is responsible to God for responding to that God-consciousness within him. Furthermore, God has given the Bible as His instruction manual for mankind. Let me emphasize here that the Word of God—the Bible—is not a secular book that can be properly interpreted by secular minds. To benefit the Church and the world, Jesus appoints, from among His followers, apostles, prophets, evangelists, shepherds, and teachers, so that all may come into the knowledge and understanding of the truth of God's Word.

And he gave some, apostles; and some, prophets; and some, evangelists; and some, pastors

and teachers; For the perfecting of the saints,
for the work of the ministry, for the edifying of
the body of Christ: Till we all come in the unity
of the faith, and of the knowledge of the Son of
God, unto a perfect man, unto the measure of
the stature of the fulness of Christ:
—Ephesians 4:11–13

These officers are specially endowed, spiritually, to teach and to administer the Word of God. Anyone who claims to be a Christian leader but does not have the ability to administer and to lead others into the truth of the Word of God, falls short of a true calling of Christ. The people under such leadership will be left wanting and can easily embrace error. Without God in our lives in a personal and practical way, we would exist without knowing what our true purpose is and how to fulfill it.

When we deviate from God's stipulated method of interpreting the Word of God, we leave ourselves open to an incorrect application of scripture and call it truth. In Christian theology, truth is not only the written Word of God. Truth is also the person of Jesus Christ. Jesus Christ is "The Way" to God, "The Truth" of God and "The Life" of God.

Jesus saith unto him, I am the way, the truth,
and the life: no man cometh unto the Father,
but by me. If ye had known me, ye should have

known my Father also: and from henceforth ye
know him, and have seen him.

—John 14:6–7

Any belief that is not centered solely upon a relationship with the person of Jesus Christ could never lead one to a relationship with the Father or qualify him to enter into the kingdom of Heaven when his spirit leaves his body at death.

Today, relationship with Jesus Christ, the Father, and the Holy Spirit has been largely replaced by religious thinking and practices. This is the genius of Satan to derail the Church, distort Christianity, and give man a deceptive alternative to a relationship with God. Over the centuries, the shift from relationship to religion has taken root in the hearts and minds of the masses, and religion is accepted as God's way for man's sins to be forgiven and for man to get to God. Religions are now in the thousands, each with its individual belief and practices, claiming to get man to Heaven when he dies, but, ironically, they all contradict God's prescribed way.

∽∽∽

Chapter 3

Distorting Truths

❦

Religion does not determine how man
gets to heaven. God does.

❦

Religiosity seems to always find a way of complicating the things God has made simple for us to understand and to relate to. For example, Jesus Christ said that unless a man is born again he can neither see, nor can he enter into, the Kingdom of Heaven, and He gave an illustration of how this happens.

> Jesus answered and said unto him, Verily, verily, I say unto thee, Except a man be born again, he cannot see the kingdom of God.⁴ Nicodemus saith unto him, How can a man be born when he is old? can he enter the second time into his mother's womb, and be born?⁵ Jesus answered, Verily, verily, I say unto thee, Except a man be born of water and of the Spirit, he cannot enter

into the kingdom of God.⁶ That which is born of the flesh is flesh; and that which is born of the Spirit is spirit.⁷ Marvel not that I said unto thee, Ye must be born again.⁸ The wind bloweth where it listeth, and thou hearest the sound thereof, but canst not tell whence it cometh, and whither it goeth: so is every one that is born of the Spirit.
—John 3:3–8

Nothing in this statement could be misunderstood. Religious minds, however, would not accept this simple statement of fact. Religious minds want to give their own input and have their own ideas included in order to have a stake in God's government on the earth. Those with a religious spirit intermingle their own agenda with God's agenda, and in so doing, they get man to believe their distorted ideas.

They add things like: *"All roads lead to Rome . . . Our beliefs are not the same but we all serve the same God . . . There are different ways to get to God and to Heaven."*

There is absolutely no truth or intelligence in any of these statements yet billions prefer to believe these senseless sayings rather than believe the One who knows and is Himself Truth. If you get on an airplane destined for the United States from anywhere in the world, would it take you to Rome? Further, consider this: would God be a part of every conflicting and opposing doctrine, when **all** purport to get men to heaven? Would He endorse the aggressive competition for men's souls which causes quarrels, fights, rivalries, and even wars? Would God use those ungodly ways and acts? No. God is never a part of these ideas, beliefs and practices. Demons are. Their aim is to distract from the God-ordained way through which man can be saved from his sins and get to Heaven—that is, through the person of Jesus Christ. Misplaced truths are commonly accepted as truths just as misplaced righteousness is commonly accepted as righteousness. These misplaced truths have succeeded in turning much of Christianity into religion. What a mighty blow Satan, working through religion, has dealt to Christianity, taking away its power and influence in the world.

There are yet other examples of widely accepted distorted truths. Let us look at some others.

"You work to earn your salvation in order to gain entrance into Heaven." There is absolutely no truth in this. God's Word says, "For by grace are ye saved through faith; and that not of yourselves; it is the gift of God: Not of works, lest any man should boast" (Ephesians 2:8–9). It further states, "Behold the Lamb of God which taketh away the sin of the world" (John 1:29). And, "Neither is there salvation in any other: for there is none other name under heaven given among men, whereby we must be saved" (Acts 4:12).

These and other scriptures render "salvation by works" false. So too is salvation by any other means that is contrary to God's way. God said that man's righteousness is as "filthy rags." Why then would anyone think that their filthy rags—the works of their own sinful hands—would earn them a place in Heaven? Let God be true and every man a liar.

> *But we are all as an unclean thing, and all our righteousness are as filthy rags; and we all do fade as a leaf; and our iniquities, like the wind, have taken us away.*
>
> *—Isaiah 64:6*

> *God forbid: yea, let God be true, but every man a liar; as it is written, That thou mightest be justified in thy sayings, and mightest overcome when thou art judged.*
>
> *—Romans: 3:4*

Religion does not determine how man gets to heaven. God does. God gives every man the right to choose between Him and anything or anyone else, and this choice decides our hereafter. His Word alone instructs us on how to get to His heaven and there is grave danger in distorting God's Word, in misrepresenting God, and in practicing beliefs that are not of God.

֍

Salvation is never earned.

֍

If man could obtain righteousness and also earn salvation by his supposed "good works," why did Jesus Christ come to earth and suffer all that He did to pay the ultimate penalty for sin through the sacrifice of His life? Why would He shed His blood to make atonement for man's sins, and then support a belief that promises salvation through our good works?

What religious acts did the Samaritan woman, who Jesus met at Jacob's well, have to perform to be forgiven of her sins? What religious acts did the men who she brought to meet Jesus have to perform to receive their salvation? All they had to do was to repent of their sins and, by the act of their faith, receive Jesus Christ into their hearts as their personal Savior and Lord, and salvation was theirs—no rituals, no ceremonies and no religion. This is all anyone has to do. Salvation is never earned. Salvation is a gift from God to the sinner who gives his or her heart to Jesus Christ in genuine repentance for their sins. God's gift to man is Jesus Christ.

> *Then saith the woman of Samaria unto him, How is it that thou, being a Jew, askest drink of me, which am a woman of Samaria? for the Jews have no dealings with the Samaritans.*[10] *Jesus answered and said unto her, If thou knewest the gift of God, and who it is that saith to thee, Give me to drink; thou wouldest have asked of him, and he would have given thee living water.*
>
> *—John 4:9–10*

The recipient of a gift is not a joint provider of the gift. A gift is given freely to the recipient as an expression of love.

> *For God so loved the world, that he gave his only begotten Son, that whosoever believeth in him should not perish, but have everlasting life.*
> —John 3:16

> *For by grace are ye saved through faith; and that not of yourselves; it is the gift of God:* [9] *Not of works, lest any man should boast.*
> —Ephesians 2:8–9

No one could lay claim to having any part in the purchase of our salvation, a salvation which Jesus Christ alone made available, and which God gives freely to the repentant sinner. If anyone could have, then Jesus Christ's work of redemption would be a sham. Which religious leader, with all his doctrines and religious practices, shared in the sufferings, death, burial, and resurrection of Jesus Christ, to give him a claim to self-inclusion in the salvation of man?

With the absence of Truth, this is what takes place in religious minds.

Religious leaders tell us they would act as our mediator and pray in our stead so that we might gain right standing with God, rather than encouraging us to go to God through the only mediator, Jesus Christ.

Religious minds want to claim the responsibility for man's salvation and have come up with so many ways to take our focus away from Jesus Christ to their brand of religion.

Some religions teach their followers to pray to those who are dead so that the dead could, in turn, pray to God on their behalf. Others teach their followers to pray to those they believe have more favor with Jesus, so that Jesus would grant their petition through those persons. These are clear examples of how religion tampers with the minds and sensibilities of those who are prone to following anyone and anything other than God's way— Jesus Christ. Every religion has its prescribed, distorted way of getting to Heaven but God has only one way of getting to Heaven. God's way is given in His Word, the Bible, and it is our responsibility to allow the Spirit of Truth to open our understanding of the Word of God, and to keep it in absolute context to gain the benefits from its authenticity.

How must Jesus Christ feel after He has sacrificed Himself to provide salvation for mankind, then to watch man devise his own plan of salvation and convince others to embrace it! By this, religious leaders are saying that God's way is wrong and their way is right. God does not overlook this, as most presume.

> *But though we, or an angel from heaven, preach any other gospel unto you than that which we have preached unto you, let him be accursed.* [9]

As we said before, so say I now again, if any man preach any other gospel unto you than that ye have received, let him be accursed.

—Galatians 1:8–9

God is grieved at the presumption of the religious who dare to advance their distortions as His truth and who cause men's souls to be damned forever.

It is a gross misconception to expect one to attain to God's righteousness through the practice of religion, when religion and God's way radically oppose each other. Religious practices deny one relationship with God and could only result in misplaced righteousness.

Chapter 4

"Religionizing" Relationship

Relationship with God the Father has been replaced with religion, with its legalistic ideas, concepts, and doctrines and, as a consequence, man has lost his way. Consider the concepts of family—father, mother, brother, sister, relatives—and even of friendship, which are based on relationship. If you try to introduce rigid, legalistic practices into these relationships, eventually the love, freedom and oneness that formed the basis for relationship would be lost. The once beautiful relationships they enjoyed with each other would now be based on rules and rituals—do's and don'ts—and the relationships would corrode because loving one another would no longer be the basis of these relationships. This is precisely what the introduction of religion into Christianity has done. Jesus Christ spoke of this in His parable.

> *Another parable spake he unto them; The kingdom of heaven is like unto leaven, which a woman took, and hid in three measures of meal, till the whole was leavened.*
>
> —*Matthew 13:33*

Leaven, more commonly known as yeast, is used in the Bible as a symbol of evil. Like leaven, religion has subtly and insidiously crept into Christ's Christianity, multiplying until it is found throughout the Church. Unfortunately, this perversion is now widely accepted as Christianity. However, the Church and the world are without excuse because the Father and Jesus Christ have given us Their Word and the Spirit of Truth to lead and to guide us into all truths. If we reject the knowledge that God has given to us, He would also reject us. We would then be left without a relationship with Him, with Jesus, or with the Holy Spirit, and we would be left wondering, "Where is God?" God's Word is not subject to alteration or change. It stands forever.

Religion is grievous to God—not because God is affected by it, but because His children are affected by it.

God made us. He takes delight in us (Revelation 4:11). He refers to us as "the apple of His eye" and as His greatest work of art—His masterpiece. Would God then introduce religion into our lives to take our focus from Him—from loving, obeying, reverencing, and worshipping Him—and cause us to put our focus and faith on another? Has not religion tampered with the mind, corrupted man's thinking, and hampered his relationship with his Maker? Religion is grievous to God—not because God is affected by it, but because His children are affected by it. As the loving Father that He is, He grieves for His children, knowing that they have chosen the way of separation from Him by choosing religion instead of Him. In God's loving kindness towards us, He is always working and reaching out to man to bring him back to Him so that man, once again, could bring joy and pleasure to his Maker. He reaches out to us so that we might escape the horrors of eternal separation from Him, which cannot be reversed, in spite of religion's claim.

When anyone, who once traded relationship with God for religion, chooses to return to God, the Father's arms are always waiting to welcome him home. Many have come back and many are still coming back to a loving welcome from the Father, Who forgives the repentant. His love and mercy never run out.

Take note of how God dealt with Israel. You will see in our discourse later that Israel's offense was so great that it caused God to turn His back on their religious practices and shut His ears to their lengthy and pious prayers. His resulting rebuke to them was sharp and left no room for rebuttal.

> *Bring no more vain oblations; incense is an abomination unto me; the new moons and sabbaths, the calling of assemblies, I cannot away*

with; it is iniquity, even the solemn meeting. [14] *Your new moons and your appointed feasts my soul hateth: they are a trouble unto me; I am weary to bear them.* [15] *And when ye spread forth your hands, I will hide mine eyes from you: yea, when ye make many prayers, I will not hear: your hands are full of blood.*

—Isaiah1:13–15

Yet we hear God's heart. His purpose and His intentions were revealed in His impassioned plea to the Israelites, as He yearned for them to turn away from their sins and come back to Him.

Come now, and let us reason together, saith the LORD: though your sins be as scarlet, they shall be as white as snow; though they be red like crimson, they shall be as wool.

—Isaiah 1:18

This is relationship! This is God! This is the way God deals with sinful man. He longs for man's return to Him. This is love and love is redemptive!

Chapter 5

Righteousness — What is it Really?

The debate on what righteousness is has produced scores of responses, thoughts, ideas, and opinions. Some have produced and used emblems to signify righteousness. Some have adopted certain vocal tones to express their version of righteousness. Some have worn special types of garments while others have taken on certain postures. Many have adopted rules and policies to attain to righteousness and there are yet other forms. The solution to this very simple, though seemingly puzzling, issue is deduced from the Word of God.

Righteousness is simply being in right standing with God.

Righteousness has nothing to do with the emblems, forms and rituals mentioned above. Again, these ideas come from the failure to apply the formula God has given in His Word to understand doctrine and gain knowledge of biblical truths and principles (Isaiah 28:9–10).

Any assumed knowledge and interpretation of the Bible that has not come through this process needs to be examined. Failure to do this has brought chaos, and derailment of truth and sound doctrine.

What brings a person into right standing with God? It is his unmovable, unshakable faith, love, and obedience to God and His Word, nurtured through relationship with Jesus Christ. Where these virtues are found, God, Jesus Christ and the Holy Spirit are the Authors and Orchestrators of them. When an individual understands this, he allows God to be God in his life, giving Him complete control, regardless of how God decides to work in and through him. It is only when God is satisfied that these virtues have been shaped in an individual that he qualifies to have God impute His righteousness in his heart and life. God is the Author and Finisher of the faith of those who have attained to His righteousness. Man in himself, through the performance of rituals, forms, and religious do's and don'ts, cannot attain to righteousness. If he could, then why would God say that man's righteousness is as "filthy rags" (Isaiah 64:6) and that, "There is none righteous, no not one" (Romans 3:10)? No man can claim equality with Him or entertain any thought of shared responsibility for man's godly virtues. This is what religion tries to do.

֍

True righteousness comes only from God.

֍

John the Baptist had the proper understanding of how man receives divine virtues such as righteousness. When approached by the religious leaders who wanted to create rivalry between him and Jesus, John seized the opportunity to give them a most profound and fundamental truth that all men in all times should learn and never forget. This is a truth that is the very foundation needed in order to receive divine virtues from God; a truth that would eliminate the useless exertion that religious men put themselves and their followers through, which has no value to God. John's response was, "A man can receive nothing except it be given him from heaven" (John 3:27). Herein is the answer to how one attains to righteousness, as well as every other godly virtue. True righteousness comes only from God. Scripture supports this conclusively. If God had intended for man to acquire his own righteousness and other godly virtues, He would have sanctioned any idea and practice that man might conceive. Man must not forget the fact that he is fallen and needs Jesus **at all times**, for He is the only one through whom man can receive anything from God. I make this statement in New Testament terms.

When I was a young Christian, my love and passion for Jesus Christ and the Father burned within me constantly. I needed all that the Word of God had promised me in order to please Jesus and the Father. The more Jesus and the Holy Spirit poured into me, the more I hungered after Them. I knew this was not my doing, that it was all Their doing to feed my spirit and soul, to build me up spiritually, and to make me a Christian, a true child of God. Even from my spiritual infancy I knew that there was nothing inherently good in me, and this was confirmed later in the Word of God (Romans 7:18). I knew that if I had bad thoughts, they came from the deposits of my fallen nature or from the devil, and if I had good thoughts, they came from the Father, Jesus, or the Holy Spirit. Providentially, I was given the gift of discernment to know Who in the Trinity was speaking to me and teaching me at every given time. I was growing spiritually at a fast rate, and the time came when I wanted to be righteous to ensure that my life was pleasing to the Trinity. I wasted no time thinking that I had the answer, but I pleaded with the Father and Jesus, through tears and supplication, to make me righteous. Within a few minutes the Father's voice said to me, "Romans 10:1–4." I immediately rose up from my knees and went to the scripture, and there was the answer to my pleading. Over time, the study of the Word of God expanded this answer which the Father had given to me out of the scriptures.

Brethren, my heart's desire and prayer to God for Israel is, that they might be saved.[2] For I bear them record that they have a zeal of God, but not according to knowledge.[3] For they being ignorant of God's righteousness, and going about to establish their own righteousness, have not submitted themselves unto the righteousness of God.[4] For Christ is the end of the law for righteousness to every one that believeth.

—Romans 10:1–4

Religious minds that are unlearned in the Word of God cumber and exert themselves about things they can never attain of themselves. When God called Abraham to walk before Him and be perfect, Abraham was not a righteous man, but after God orchestrated Abraham's faith, obedience, and love for Him, God then imputed His righteousness to Abraham. Many desire to become righteous and go about establishing their own righteousness, not knowing that righteousness is imputed by God and is not of oneself.

Chapter 6

Job's Attempt to Establish Righteousness

❧❧

True righteousness does not draw
attention to itself, nor does it lord
itself over others.

❧❧

The Bible tells of Job who every day made sacrifices for himself in order to maintain his righteousness before God, and to attain righteousness for his family. Job, like most, did not yet comprehend what righteousness is to God, so Job went about establishing his own righteousness. Job meant well but God, through Job's experiences, proved to Job—and to us all—that his perception of righteousness was not in keeping with what God determines as righteousness.

In the eyes of God, Job was indeed a righteous man, **not because of his sacrifices** but because of his **absolute, unshakable and unmovable faith in God and in**

God's ways and principles. Job in his meekness, however, did This is so characteristic of true righteousness.
True righteousness does not "ring its own bell." True
righteousness does not "wave a flag" to draw attention
to itself, nor does it lord itself over others.

Because of Job's righteousness, God knew He could
use Job as an example for all of mankind to learn that it
is loyalty to God that would merit God's righteousness,
particularly loyalty that is sustained under adverse cir-
cumstances. God, in His infinite wisdom, enlisted Satan
to accomplish this divine plan and, as a result, all that
Job had feared suddenly took place. Job lost all of his
worldly possessions, his health, and even his treasured
children who were the main emphasis of his numerous
sacrifices before God.

> And there was a day when his sons and his
> daughters were eating and drinking wine in
> their eldest brother's house: [14] And there came
> a messenger unto Job, and said, The oxen were
> plowing, and the asses feeding beside them: [15]
> And the Sabeans fell upon them, and took them
> away; yea, they have slain the servants with
> the edge of the sword; and I only am escaped
> alone to tell thee. [16] While he was yet speaking,
> there came also another, and said, The fire of
> God is fallen from heaven, and hath burned
> up the sheep, and the servants, and consumed
> them; and I only am escaped alone to tell

thee. ¹⁷ While he was yet speaking, there came also another, and said, The Chaldeans made out three bands, and fell upon the camels, and have carried them away, yea, and slain the servants with the edge of the sword; and I only am escaped alone to tell thee. ¹⁸ While he was yet speaking, there came also another, and said, Thy sons and thy daughters were eating and drinking wine in their eldest brother's house: ¹⁹ And, behold, there came a great wind from the wilderness, and smote the four corners of the house, and it fell upon the young men, and they are dead; and I only am escaped alone to tell thee. ²⁰ Then Job arose, and rent his mantle, and shaved his head, and fell down upon the ground, and worshipped, ²¹ And said, Naked came I out of my mother's womb, and naked shall I return thither: the LORD gave, and the LORD hath taken away; blessed be the name of the LORD. ²² In all this Job sinned not, nor charged God foolishly.

—Job 1:13–22

All of Job's sacrificing of animals did not and could not impress God, nor did it make Job and his family righteous before God. God did not prescribe Job's practices for him to obtain righteousness. God had appointed the sacrificing of animals as a temporary means, a foreshadowing, in anticipation of the sacrifice of His Son Who would come to earth to shed His blood and give His life as that ultimate and perfect sacrifice for man's sins. If, in the course of making such sacrifices, man would put his confidence and faith in the **act**—as Job did for the righteousness of his family—that would be displeasing to God.

⁂

> Virtue is not in the outward act but in the inward heart condition...not in the 'doing' but in the 'being'.

⁂

The people of God must know that even when God endorses an outward practice, like He did with Job and the children of Israel, unless that practice is absolutely motivated by love and by faith in God, and in Jesus Christ, it only stands as a barrier between them and God, and does not qualify them for righteousness. God knew Job's heart and credited him for his lifelong loyalty to Him, which was even more evident during Job's many hardships. Job's faith and love for God never waned through it all. Job had, in ignorance, placed emphasis on sacrifices to gain righteousness, but God used Job's experiences to highlight the fact that the true virtue is not in the practice itself, but in one's absolute love, faith and obedience to God which renders the individual worthy to have God's righteousness imputed to him. The virtue is not in the outward act but in the inward heart condition that propels the act. The virtue is not in the 'doing' but in the 'being'. When we are in relationship with God, we willingly make sacrifices for Him, out of our love for Him. God readily accepts such sacrifices which emerge from relationship with Him rather than those which are propelled by man's ideas and in which God is not central.

We also have much to learn about righteousness and what it is not from Eliphaz, Bildad and Zophar, Job's closest friends. When they saw Job's sufferings, they appointed themselves Job's judge, and judged him guilty of secret sins. They were sure that God was now exposing Job's sins for all to see. They took it upon themselves to act as spokesmen for God, debated Job's professed innocence, and spoke with such confidence and pride in their discovery of Job's "secret sins." This was their opportunity to show their righteousness above Job's. They were ignorant of the fact that they themselves were unrighteous before God by committing the sin of judging Job, and that God was taking note of it. When God had had enough of their false righteousness and judgments of His servant, Job, and of their misrepresentation of Him, God put a stop to it. God ordered Eliphaz, Bildad and Zophar to repent before His servant, Job, for having judged him, and to request Job's prayer so that God would not pour out His fierce wrath upon them. Was their sin of judging God's servant, Job, so grievous to God? Apparently it was.

*And it was so, that after the L*ORD *had spoken these words unto Job, the L*ORD *said to Eliphaz the Temanite, My wrath is kindled against thee, and against thy two friends: for ye have not spoken of me the thing that is right, as my servant Job hath. ⁸ Therefore take unto you now seven bullocks and seven rams, and go to my servant Job, and offer up for yourselves a burnt offering; and my servant Job shall pray for you: for him will I accept: lest I deal with you after your folly, in that ye have not spoken of me the thing which is right, like my servant Job. ⁹ So Eliphaz the Temanite and Bildad the Shuhite and Zophar the Naamathite went, and did according as the L*ORD *commanded them:*

—Job 42:7-9

Fortunately for them, the sin of pride did not stand in their way of going to Job to ask for his forgiveness and prayer. Because Job was indeed a righteous man, he forgave them and prayed for them, and, as a result, they were spared from God's wrath.

*And the L*ORD *turned the captivity of Job, when he prayed for his friends: also the L*ORD *gave Job twice as much as he had before.¹¹ Then came there unto him all his brethren, and all his sisters, and all they that had been of his acquaintance before, and did eat bread with him in his*

house: and they bemoaned him, and comforted
him over all the evil that the LORD had brought
upon him: every man also gave him a piece of
money, and every one an earring of gold.[12] *So the*
LORD blessed the latter end of Job more than his
beginning: for he had fourteen thousand sheep,
and six thousand camels, and a thousand yoke
of oxen, and a thousand she asses.[13] *He had also*
seven sons and three daughters.

—Job 42:10–13

God delivered Job from his affliction, and blessed him abundantly, restoring to him over and above all that he had lost.

Perhaps God spared the lives of Eliphaz, Bildad and Zophar because they might have been good to Job before they had committed this great sin of judging him. Most likely, in Job's recovery he would need his friends and, Job may have experienced much sorrow at not having them. More importantly, Job's friends would have had a lifelong lesson which they would pass on to their wives, children, family, friends and communities, to caution them from the great sin of judging others, and to teach them to leave judgment to God. This lesson would be propagated for the good of future generations. May we too learn this vital lesson.

God does not always settle the issue of judging others in the way he settled it with Eliphaz, Bildad and Zophar. It is often settled through unanswered prayers in the face of sickness, disease, disappointment, failure and other misfortunes. Sometimes God settles it with premature death. Lives are shortened when men tamper with God's servants and God's work, but it seems not to matter because the blindness that has come over the religious is so great. Christians, beware of this! Beware of practicing the sin of self-righteous judgment. Church leaders, in particular, must be careful not to engage in the judgment of others and pass this ungodly practice on to their congregations in the name of righteousness. This is misplaced righteousness and it is blight to the Body of Christ, and Jesus Christ is very grieved by it.

Christians who practice this sin are plagued with all manner of ills and misfortunes, and are denied of the promises of God which are reserved for the faithful and righteous. The Church is in urgent need of the Spirit of Truth to quell Satan's onslaught of misplaced righteousness that has become a cancer and a putrefying sore in the Body of Christ. If the Holy Spirit would open one's eyes to the endless list of misplaced truths in the Body of Christ, sincere Christians would fall on their faces before God in sackcloth and ashes and beg the Lord for His mercy and forgiveness.

You have heard of the old adage, "the pot calling the kettle black," or, as my mother often said it, "the pot telling the kettle that its bottom is black." When adherence to the Word of God is practiced once again that proverbial pot would cease to accuse the kettle that its bottom is black. Rather, the pot would first examine its own bottom, and, discovering that it too is black, would clean it; then, with genuine concern, it would, in turn, reach out with loving hands to help the kettle clean its black bottom.

If men understood God's ways and His infinite wisdom, they would speak less about what they do not know. They would not presume to know what God is doing with or through others. They would let God be God.

God's thoughts and ways are not man's thoughts and ways. Religious men like to think that they could help God deal with what they consider the sins and unrighteousness of others. In fact, they are ignorant of God's ways. Even though they are not conscious of their own sins and their unrighteousness, they are, nevertheless, offensive to God. Such practices grieve God and are a victory for Satan and his kingdom.

Chapter 7

Israel's Practice of Misplaced Righteousness

*I*srael had been practicing misplaced righteousness before God for a long time, and the day came when God could not take it anymore. When God, who is patient and long-suffering, said that He had had enough, one can imagine just how bad it had become to Him. With much grief, God summoned heaven and earth as His witnesses before He acted.

> *The vision of Isaiah the son of Amoz, which he saw concerning Judah and Jerusalem in the days of Uzziah, Jotham, Ahaz, and Hezekiah, kings of Judah.² Hear, O heavens, and give ear, O earth: for the* Lord *hath spoken, I have nourished and brought up children, and they have rebelled against me.*
>
> —*Isaiah 1:1–2*

God then expressed His displeasure about it to the prophet, Isaiah, and sent him to the people with His rebuke.

I want you to imagine the faces of the proud priests and religious hierarchy when Isaiah went to Israel with God's reprimand, and bellowed out God's hatred and displeasure of what they had put their confidence in to obtain righteousness:

The ox knoweth his owner, and the ass his master's crib: but Israel doth not know, my people doth not consider.[4] Ah sinful nation, a people laden with iniquity, a seed of evildoers, children that are corrupters: they have forsaken the LORD, *they have provoked the Holy One of Israel unto anger, they are gone away backward.[5] Why should ye be stricken any more? ye will revolt more and more: the whole head is sick, and the whole heart faint.[6] From the sole of the foot even unto the head there is no soundness in it; but wounds, and bruises, and putrifying sores: they have not been closed, neither bound up, neither mollified with ointment.[7] Your country is desolate, your cities are burned with fire: your land, strangers devour it in your presence, and it is desolate, as overthrown by strangers.[8] And the daughter of Zion is left as a cottage in a vineyard, as a lodge in a garden of cucumbers, as a besieged city.[9] Except the* LORD *of hosts had left unto us a very small remnant, we should have been as Sodom, and we should have been like unto Gomorrah.[10] Hear the word of the* LORD, *ye rulers of Sodom; give ear unto the law of our God, ye people of Gomorrah.*[11]*To what purpose is the multitude of your sacrifices unto me? saith the LORD: I am full of the burnt offerings of rams, and the fat of fed beasts; and I delight not in the blood of bullocks, or of lambs, or of he goats.*[12]*When ye come to appear before me, who hath required this at your hand, to tread my courts?*[13]*Bring no more vain oblations; incense is an abomination unto me; the new moons and sabbaths, the calling of assemblies, I cannot away with; it is iniquity, even the solemn meeting.*[14]*Your new moons and your appointed feasts my soul hateth: they are a trouble unto me; I am weary to bear them.*[15]*And when ye spread forth your hands, I will hide mine eyes from you: yea, when ye make many prayers, I will not hear: your hands are full of blood.*

—Isaiah 1:3–15

In spite of His disgust with His people, God still reached out, offering them a way to redirect their steps and correct their course:

Wash you, make you clean; put away the evil of your doings from before mine eyes; cease to do evil;[17] *Learn to do well; seek judgment, relieve the oppressed, judge the fatherless, plead for the widow.*[18]*Come now, and let us reason together,*

saith the LORD: though your sins be as scarlet,
they shall be as white as snow; though they be
red like crimson, they shall be as wool
—Isaiah 1:16–18

What was the value of their sacrificing of thousands of animals, their keeping of new moons, feasts, solemn assemblies, and Sabbaths, which they had kept all these years? They were of no value to God or to them, but they did not know it. They believed that these rituals could establish their righteousness before God, and they therefore practiced them religiously. They prided themselves on their ability to perform them, and considered themselves righteous. Yet, all this time, God so hated their practices that He turned His back towards them and shut his ears from their prayers. Yes, it was God who had sanctioned these animal sacrifices. I understand your dilemma here, so let me help you with it. The practice of sacrificing animals was sanctioned by God under the Old Covenant as a temporary measure until He would send Jesus Christ as His perfect, one-time sacrifice to pay for the sins of mankind. Even so, God never intends that anything He sanctions should replace Him in the hearts of His people. Anyone or anything which replaces God becomes an obstacle to relationship between God and that individual. When we place more value on ordinances rather than on relationship with God, God sees that as a rejection of Him.

Men have left God for religion.
They have pursued anointing, good
preaching, power, fame, and mammon
at the expense of an intimate
relationship with God.

God's lamentation before Isaiah was very emotional and quite telling. It highlighted His yearning for relationship as opposed to the religious rituals offered to Him by Israel. God said to them that the ox knows its master and the ass knows its feeding trough. The ox and the ass know where to go to get their sustenance to remain alive, but His people, Israel, do not know to come to Him—their God, Master, Source, and Sustainer—to maintain their relationship with Him, for their nourishment and the preservation of their lives. Instead, they put their trust in ordinances and sacrifices. What an indictment on the people of God. God was saying that the animals had exhibited more intelligence than His people. My God! This is what has happened to the Church and the world, and this is what would bring its own judgment. Men have left God for religion. They have pursued anointing, good preaching, power, fame, and mammon at the expense of an intimate relationship with God and this is working against them in ways they cannot see.

The result is sickness, disease, wars, and untold suffering, and men then accuse God of causing these ills instead of blaming themselves. What a job the "Master Deceiver," Satan, has pulled off on mankind . . . even on the people of God.

When God warns His children of the sins they are committing, it is wise for them to stop committing those sins, repent and turn back to God. He is merciful and long-suffering but, if they continue in sin, He breaks in on them in a way that is not pleasant. God reserves the right to do that. God has not given that right to self-righteous men, but self-righteous men take it upon themselves to play God, and some have the audacity to say that God "told them" and that God "sent them," when He did not. God does not send men who have wrong hearts to speak on His behalf—men with their own prideful, selfish, and self-serving agendas and motives. Many are trapped by the "God said" fad that is plaguing the Church. Most of what they declare that God said does not line up with His Word and His will, and they therefore deceive and mislead those who believe their claims. If, however, the people of God fail to measure what is said against the character of Jesus Christ and the truth of His Word, they will be moved by these fads because religiosity always appeals to self and to the flesh, and therefore gets the attention.

Unmistakably, as depicted in His response towards His people Israel, God wants relationship and not religious indulgences. He wants man's heart, his love, his faith, and his obedience. He wants to be our Father and wants us to be His children.

I love God simply because He is God—my God. I love the way He orchestrates my life and how He expresses the "fruit" of His Spirit toward me. It is in this way that I, in turn, have learned to do the same to others. I love God for His excellence in how He does things. He is as dramatic as he is passionate. He is perfect in love and in judgment.

Chapter 8

Violators of Righteousness

Self-righteous individuals believe that they are helping God to discover unrighteousness in others. When they think they have discovered someone who does not live up to what they assume to be righteousness, they begin to criticize, chastise, condemn, gossip, slander, and altogether violate the very principles of righteousness which they claim to be upholding. To those individuals, sins like hatred, envy, jealousy, lies, division, greed, pride, distorting scripture to suit themselves, and judging others are not regarded as sin, and do not apply to them. Yet, these are the very sins that God considers most grievous and deadly—an abomination to Him.

> These six things doth the LORD hate: yea, seven are an abomination unto him:[17]A proud look, a lying tongue, and hands that shed innocent blood,[18]An heart that deviseth wicked imaginations, feet that be swift in running to mischief,[19]A false witness that speaketh lies, and he that soweth discord among brethren.
>
> —Proverbs 6:16–19

This is the degree to which Satan has gained control of religious minds and warped their thinking.

Self-righteous individuals often step beyond the boundaries that the Word of God has given to men. They step into areas that Jesus Christ and the Father have reserved for Themselves. This presumption causes men to see themselves as "judge, jury, and executioner" of others.

I must again refer to my mother's favorite saying, that the pot tells the kettle that its bottom is black. The pot and the kettle sit on the same fireplace and both their bottoms are black. The pot sees that the bottom of the kettle is black, but ironically, does not see that its own bottom is black. This is the kind of judgment that is practiced in some Christian churches in the name of righteousness when, in fact, it is false or misplaced righteousness. For one to assume that they know God's ways when they do not, and then pass on their misinformation about God, is a serious matter. When religious leaders claim to know how God is working in the life of another, and then go on to make their unrighteous judgments, they cause serious damage to their followers and to those who look up to them, as well as to those looking on from outside the Christian circle. This then becomes a case of the blind leading the blind. It is no wonder that the ditches are filled with blind and misguided Christians.

ֆ֍

Religious men who claim to be ambassadors for Christ, but do not have the redemptive spirit and nature of Christ, deceive themselves and others.

ֆ֍

If God were to disassociate Himself from every child of His who sins, like Abraham, Moses, David and all else, God would end up alone without any children because all have sinned and come short of the glory of God (Romans 3:23).

When the pot accepts the fact that its bottom is also black, it would no longer judge and accuse the kettle of the fact that its bottom is black. In its false, self-righteous judgments, it thinks itself wise, when it is, in fact, a fool. Throughout the Bible, righteous men, on occasions, have committed unrighteous acts. These unrighteous acts did not make them unrighteous men in the eyes of God. The conviction that their unrighteous acts had grieved God drove them to their knees in repentance and to a hasty return to God, having learnt new things from these experiences. God, in His omniscience uses these experiences to forge in His people a deeper love, obedience, and commitment to God. Through it all, He teaches them His ways for the benefit of others. David was such a man. He murdered

Uriah, the Hittite, so that he could have his wife, yet David was considered by God to be a "man after His own heart" (1 Samuel 13:14). On having been convicted that he had offended God by committing such an unrighteous act, David hastened back to God in sackcloth and ashes. Psalm 51, penned by David himself, reveals a broken and repentant heart, one filled with faith and love toward God, and a passion to always be pleasing and in right standing with Him.

God is Love. Love is redemptive. Religious men who claim to be ambassadors for Christ, but do not have the redemptive spirit and nature of Christ, deceive themselves and others. Jesus said that we will know them by their "fruit"—that is to say, by the characteristics and actions they display. Jesus Christ does not appoint as ambassadors, men whose spirit, character, and agenda are contrary to His. God's ambassadors must have the wisdom of the Holy Spirit to properly represent Christ and implement His agenda on the earth. Christ's agenda is to save, restore, reconcile, and redeem. If we fail to operate in that spirit, we are in fact operating in unrighteousness and God's Word is clear on the matter:

> *Rejoice not when thine enemy falleth, and let not thine heart be glad when he stumbleth:* [18]
> *Lest the* Lord *see it, and it displease him, and he turn away his wrath from him.*
>
> —*Proverbs 24:17–18*

Brethren, if a man be overtaken in a fault, ye which are spiritual, restore such an one in the spirit of meekness; considering thyself, lest thou also be tempted.[2] Bear ye one another's burdens, and so fulfil the law of Christ.[3] For if a man think himself to be something, when he is nothing, he deceiveth himself.

—Galatians 6:1–3

He that saith he is in the light, and hateth his brother, is in darkness even until now.[10] He that loveth his brother abideth in the light, and there is none occasion of stumbling in him.[11] But he that hateth his brother is in darkness, and walketh in darkness, and knoweth not whither he goeth, because that darkness hath blinded his eyes.

—1 John 2:9–11

If a man say, I love God, and hateth his brother, he is a liar: for he that loveth not his brother whom he hath seen, how can he love God whom he hath not seen?

—1 John 4:20

For if ye forgive men their trespasses, your heavenly Father will also forgive you:[15] But if ye forgive not men their trespasses, neither will your Father forgive your trespasses.

—Matthew 6:14–15

To take a position that is contrary to the Word of God is, in itself, sin and unrighteousness, but religious spirits prevent their victims from adopting God's Word and God's way. These victims then become obsessed with the "executioner's axe." God's ways are restoration, reconciliation, and redemption. Any practice of or claim to Christianity that is contrary to restoration, reconciliation, and redemption is the practice of false Christianity, regardless of who it comes from, clergy or laity.

God's ways are restoration, reconciliation, and redemption.

Chapter 9

The Way of the Self-Righteous

❧❦

Self-righteousness presents itself
as perfect—without shortcomings,
without sin, and without guilt. It looks
for sin in others but is never
conscious of its own.

❧❦

*And he spake this parable unto certain which
trusted in themselves that they were righteous,
and despised others:* ¹⁰ *Two men went up into
the temple to pray; the one a Pharisee, and the
other a publican.* ¹¹ *The Pharisee stood and
prayed thus with himself, God, I thank thee,
that I am not as other men are, extortioners,
unjust, adulterers, or even as this publican.* ¹² *I
fast twice in the week, I give tithes of all that
I possess.* ¹³ *And the publican, standing afar*

off, would not lift up so much as his eyes unto heaven, but smote upon his breast, saying, God be merciful to me a sinner. [14] I tell you, this man went down to his house justified rather than the other: for every one that exalteth himself shall be abased; and he that humbleth himself shall be exalted.

—Luke 18:9–14

The Pharisee in Jesus' parable saw himself as God's favorite and was proud to lord himself over the publican who he saw as despicable and ungodly, when, in fact, in God's eyes, it was quite the opposite. The scripture above indeed confirms that self-righteousness is self-exalting. It is self-delusionary. It presents itself as perfect—without shortcomings, without sin, and without guilt. It looks for sin in others but is never conscious of its own. Surely, self-righteousness is one of the most powerful expressions of the deceitfulness of the heart.

The self-righteous serve the purposes of Satan. They trample on others in order to draw attention to their assumed righteousness. In Christian churches, self-righteous individuals seek to build their religious popularity by identifying the sins of others. Whether vocal or silent, their intention is always to convey to others the false impression that they have no sins, or to cover up their own sins by drawing attention to the sins of others.

Self-righteous individuals are dispossessed of the true spirit of Christ that seeks to see sinners saved from their sins. Christians with self-righteous spirits deter non-Christians from making Christ their Lord and Savior, for they cause them to think that they would be pointed out, judged, labelled, and condemned for their sins, rather than forgiven, loved, and shown how to live for the Lord. Even among their fellow believers, the self-righteous reject the repentance of those who they think have sinned. The self-righteous think that they know how to diagnose the sins of others but, as is typical of such, they do not know how to prescribe or administer the corrective treatment for the sins diagnosed. Furthermore, there is no place in the thinking of self-righteous, judgmental individuals to conceive, far less to accept, that one should be forgiven, even after he has repented of his sin and is therefore back in right standing with Jesus Christ. Their passion and drive to retain the sins of others are far greater than their desire to obey God and to remit sins as Jesus commissioned His disciples to do. Yet, I hear Christ saying, "I did not come to call the righteous, but sinners to repentance" (Luke 5:32). He further says:

> *Whose soever sins ye remit, they are remitted unto them; and whose soever sins ye retain, they are retained.*
>
> *—John 20:23*

A self-righteous spirit reproduces itself in others just as the Spirit of Christ seeks to reproduce Himself

in others. In Church assemblies where this spirit oper-
ates from the pulpit, the spirits of those in the pews are
polluted. The self-righteous spirit in the Church is like a
"mother sin" that gives birth to many other sins, including the deadly sins cited in Proverbs 6:16–19. If Christ
does not move those with this spirit out of the pulpit, the
assembly would be infested with this self-righteous spirit and the Holy Spirit would depart. When this happens,
a "Saulish" spirit takes over and begins to attack assemblies where the Holy Spirit is active and demonstrating
the works of Christ. This is akin to King Saul's attacks on
David when the Spirit of the Lord departed from Saul (1
Samuel 18). Such a congregation might boast of its sin-
lessness, yet there is no spiritual life in that Church because the Holy Spirit is not there. He is not there because
the leader of the congregation has introduced contrary
spirits, and has fed to the congregation doctrines which
are opposed to Christ. Sadly, the self-righteous spirit of
the Pharisees and Sadducees is as alive and thriving in
many Christian assemblies today as it was in Jesus' day.

Chapter 10

Religious Spirits

⁂

God and Jesus Christ did not
introduce religion to man.

⁂

It should now be abundantly clear that, contrary to widely-accepted thought, God, Jesus, and the Holy Spirit are not religious. The Almighty God has no need of religion and has no religious affiliation, even if that religion professes belief in Him. Furthermore, religion can never give one access to God's heaven. It never has and it never will.

God and Jesus Christ did not introduce religion to man. It is religious spirits, assigned by Satan, that have incited man's imagination to invent this counterfeit called religion. Their diabolical purpose is to distract men from coming into relationship with God, and to rob them of the opportunity to spend eternity with Him.

These religious spirits are undoubtedly the most deceptive and deadliest of evil spirits. Look at the spiritual condition of the world. Listen to the news and read the newspaper and you would hear and see the proof of their influence. Men with religious spirits could pray pious prayers, then turn around and slaughter innocent people, use children as human shields, behead those who are not part of their religion, and commit all manner of atrocities, all in the name of their god and their religion. To think that God is in this is highly delusional. This is what religious spirits do to the mind.

Religion is Satan's most successful scheme which he masterfully engineers to appease the God-consciousness which God has placed in the heart of every individual. That God-consciousness is for man to desire God and to respond to God, not to religion. Religion's deceptive trap deludes the religious into believing that they are in a "good state", "right with God," and on their way to heaven.

In fact, religion appeals to those whose minds have been influenced to believe that religiosity impresses God, and that He sanctions it. From their skewed perspective, they see themselves better than and more righteous than others, and pride themselves in their religiosity, not realizing that it contradicts and opposes God—who He is, His Word and all that He stands for. Religion purports to represent God, but this cannot be, because God hates it. Wherever God encounters the practice of religion, He turns His back and shuts His ears to it.

Bring no more vain oblations; incense is an abomination unto me; the new moons and

> *sabbaths, the calling of assemblies, I cannot*
> *away with; it is iniquity, even the solemn meet-*
> *ing.* ¹⁴*Your new moons and your appointed*
> *feasts my soul hateth: they are a trouble unto*
> *me; I am weary to bear them.* ¹⁵*And when ye*
> *spread forth your hands, I will hide mine eyes*
> *from you: yea, when ye make many prayers, I*
> *will not hear: your hands are full of blood.*
> *—Isaiah 1:13–15*

God could not have expressed His hatred and rejection of religious practices any more forcefully than He expressed it in these passages of scripture. It is no wonder that religious spirits, working through religious minds, despise the Word of God as they do.

Jesus Christ also denounced the religionists of His day because their practices placed the people in bondages which barred them from coming to God and having a relationship with Him through Jesus Christ. Although He was born a Jew, Jesus opposed the Jewish religious leaders whose practice of their religion had become focused more on ordinances, ceremonies, rites, and rituals, rather than on relationship with God. God had instituted the laws, sacrifices, ceremonies, and ordinances of the Jewish faith. However, He did not intend that they would replace relationship with Him for He knew that these practices could not undo their sins. They were but a temporary measure, a foreshadowing of Jesus Christ, the Messiah, who would come to fulfill the requirements that these ordinances could not fulfill. He would be God's sacrifice for the fulfillment of all the laws. It would be through Jesus Christ that the people would finally come into that level of relationship which God desired of them.

Religious spirits however, had infiltrated the hierarchy of Judaism over time and overshadowed the very things that were meant to point the people to God. When Jesus saw and heard the hypocrisy of the Pharisees, Sadducees, and religious leaders, He was incensed because they were not genuinely concerned about bringing the people into a relationship with God. Instead, they were more concerned with their exalted positions, gain, and power, all the while maintaining a superficial appearance of righteousness before men.

> Then spake Jesus to the multitude, and to his disciples, ²Saying The scribes and the Pharisees sit in Moses' seat: ³All therefore whatsoever they bid you observe, that observe and do; but do not ye after their works: for they say, and do not. ⁴For they bind heavy burdens and grievous to be borne, and lay them on men's shoulders; but they themselves will not move them with one of their fingers. ⁵But all their works they do for to be seen of men: they make broad their phylacteries, and enlarge the borders of their garments, ⁶And love the uppermost rooms at feasts, and the chief seats in the synagogues,

⁷And greetings in the markets, and to be called of men, Rabbi, Rabbi.

—Matthew 23:1–7

Jesus Christ, stirred with compassion for those who were being led astray by religion, vehemently charged the religious leaders with hypocrisy.

But woe unto you, scribes and Pharisees, hypocrites! for ye shut up the kingdom of heaven against men: for ye neither go in yourselves, neither suffer ye them that are entering to go in. ¹⁴Woe unto you, scribes and Pharisees, hypocrites! for ye devour widows' houses, and for a pretence make long prayer: therefore ye shall receive the greater damnation. ¹⁵Woe unto you, scribes and Pharisees, hypocrites! for ye compass sea and land to make one proselyte, and when he is made, ye make him twofold more the child of hell than yourselves.

—Matthew 23:13–15

These leaders set themselves above everyone else, and, wearing pride like a garment, they assumed responsibility to teach the people about God and His truth. They politicized their version of truth and got the people to put their faith in their religion, rather than in God. Jesus exposed their hypocrisy, pronouncing a series of "woes" upon them, for they were the exact opposite of all that He, the Father, and the Holy Spirit stood for.

> Woe unto you, scribes and Pharisees, hypocrites! for ye pay tithe of mint and anise and cummin, and have omitted the weightier matters of the law, judgment, mercy, and faith: these ought ye to have done, and not to leave the other undone. [24]Ye blind guides, which strain at a gnat, and swallow a camel. [25]Woe unto you, scribes and Pharisees, hypocrites! for ye make clean the outside of the cup and of the platter, but within they are full of extortion and excess. [26]Thou blind Pharisee, cleanse first that which is within the cup and platter, that the outside of them may be clean also. [27]Woe unto you, scribes and Pharisees, hypocrites! for ye are like unto whited sepulchres, which indeed appear beautiful outward, but are within full of dead men's bones, and of all uncleanness. [28]Even so ye also outwardly appear righteous unto men, but within ye are full of hypocrisy and iniquity. [29]Woe unto you, scribes and Pharisees, hypocrites! because ye build the tombs of the prophets, and garnish the sepulchres of the righteous, [30]And say, If we had been in the days of our fathers, we would not have been partakers with them in the blood of the prophets.
>
> —Matthew 23:23–30

Outwardly, the scribes and Pharisees were a picture of piety, bedecked in their phylacteries and religious, priestly garments. Inwardly, they were really enemies of Jesus Christ and His truths. They charged others with failing to keep even the simplest law, yet they themselves failed to uphold what God considered "the weightier matters"—love, mercy, and truth. Jesus said they were inwardly filled with the decay of "dead men's bones," reeking of hypocrisy and self-righteousness, and thus they had committed the greater sin. They had indeed "swallowed a camel" compared to the "gnat"—that minute insect which they were so quick to accuse others of having "swallowed." Jesus' indictment on them was severe.

> *Ye serpents, ye generation of vipers, how can ye escape the damnation of hell?*
>
> —*Matthew 23:33*

I cannot say this often enough . . . the Father, Jesus Christ, and the Holy Spirit are not religionists! They are the epitome of relationship. They are lovers. They are redeemers. They are reconcilers of fallen man. God's agenda is to remit men's sins, reconcile them to Himself, and join them to one another in Christ. He has instituted repentance and forgiveness for all, even for the Christian who may stumble while on his journey towards heaven. Jesus Christ commands all Christians to do the same, particularly those who He has specially called to positions of leadership.

Religious spirits however, being counterfeiters, oppose God's plans for reconciliation. Instead, they seek to retain man's sins thereby perpetuating his separation from God, and creating division among God's people.

The religious and the self-righteous look down at the ones they think are beneath their standard of righteousness, and condemn them. They are oblivious to the fact that their condemnation of others is in direct opposition to God's Word, which seeks to redeem and to save the sinner rather than to condemn him. The reality is that they have fallen further than the ones they are condemning. This is misplaced righteousness and they do not even know it!

These self-righteous men should urgently seek to discover, through the Word of God, the power that is in the blood of Jesus Christ to remit sin—**all** sin, at **all** times. They must learn of Jesus' "seventy times seven" principle of forgiveness toward the repentant. They need to properly study the Word of God and ensure that, in quoting the Word, they apply the principle that God has given for the acquisition of knowledge and proper doctrine, rather than give themselves over to religious, self-righteous and prideful spirits. It is only then that their scriptural quotations would be in proper context.

Religious, self-righteous spirits are always accompanied by the spirits of jealousy, envy, strife, division, and a competitive spirit. This is a vicious alliance of evil spirits that may infiltrate the hearts and minds of even those who have a relationship with God through Jesus

Christ. Men who embrace these religious spirits pollute the minds of those who are unlearned in the scriptures, all the while seeking to gain attention and a place of prominence in the eyes of believers in Christ. In their push for recognition and prominence, they do not care if they unsettle the minds of the people and hinder their spiritual growth. They have no fear of God or regard for His truth, and this is highly offensive to God.

> *But whoso shall offend one of these little ones which believe in me, it were better for him that a millstone were hanged about his neck, and that he were drowned in the depth of the sea.*
> *—Matthew 18:6*

Religious, self-righteous men plot to ruin ministers and ministries which are loyal to Jesus and to the Kingdom of God. They do it as "guardians of righteousness" but care little for those who they damage or derail in the process. Like dogs, they map out territories which they claim as theirs, and fiercely guard them, to their own detriment.

When Truth came to Israel in the person of Jesus Christ, the religious leaders banded themselves together, even putting aside their differences for the sole purpose of guarding their territories against Jesus and His teachings. They had Him nailed to the cross, and thereafter, they continued persecuting His followers, relentlessly pursuing them in every town, city and village, and seeking to distort their message of salvation. This is clearly depicted in the accounts of the apostles in the book of Acts.

These religious spirits have continued to infiltrate the hearts and minds of men everywhere, and have even successfully enlisted unwitting Christians to pursue and to persecute fellow believers in assemblies where the Holy Spirit and truth are present.

The heart of the Trinity has been, and will always be, towards restoring that relationship between God and man which they had before the fall. There is nothing that Jesus Christ taught and left us in His Word that did not point to the restoration of that relationship.

Jesus came to save man from his sins. He saw that religion stood in the way of men coming to God personally for the redemption of their sins. Even His rebuke of the religious leaders was a demonstration of His passion for the salvation of men. He was prepared to go to every extent, opposing the religious hierarchy, to free and to save the souls who were held captive by religion.

It was to the religious that Jesus said:

(You) Search the scriptures; for in them ye think ye have eternal life: and they are they which testify of me. [40]*And ye will not come to me, that ye might have life.* [41]*I receive not honour from men.* [42]*But I know you, that ye have not the love of God in you.* [43]*I am come in my Father's name, and ye receive me not: if another shall come in*

his own name, him ye will receive. [44]*How can ye believe, which receive honour one of another, and seek not the honour that cometh from God only?*
—John 5:39–44

Truth, as valuable and essential as it is, more often than not, is an offense to error. Error is hostile to truth because error wants to be accepted as truth. To those who thrive on error for the purpose of controlling others, for making a name for themselves, or for power and influence, truth becomes a hindrance to them.

৵৵

Religious spirits influence people to reject truth and embrace error.

৵৵

The religious leaders professed to love the law of God but their determination to hold fast to their religious practices and doctrines proved that their love for themselves and for their own honor was greater than their love for truth, for God's honor, and for the well-being of those under their charge. It is remarkable that religion, when it becomes so entrenched in men's hearts, disregards the heart and character of God, who it professes to serve. Such is the deceitfulness of misplaced righteousness which is driven by religious spirits.

It is religious spirits that influence people to reject truth and embrace error. This is evident when we consider that it was religious spirits through which Satan worked to crucify Jesus Christ who came to earth to redeem man from the curse of sin. I urge you to beware of religious spirits and their poison spewed from the lips of men who have embraced them. Learn to discern these evil spirits disguised as the holy, the pious, and the righteous. Do not align yourself with them or entertain their distorted version of truth, for your eternal soul is at risk.

Chapter 11

From Religion to Relationship

Jesus Christ is The Way, The Truth, and The Life. Christ's Christianity therefore, is the truth that is designed to lead man on the right path to God. Religion is error and is counterfeit to The Way, The Truth, and The Life. Therefore, to associate Christ with religion is misplaced thinking and believing.

Truth and error are opposites, and when truth and error meet, there is variance. When Christ's Christianity and religion meet, there is often conflict and sometimes fatalities. Hate and love are opposites just as good and evil are, and when these meet, there is variance, opposition, tension, and unrest. When Christ and Satan meet, Satan is agitated and wants war, in spite of his knowledge of his ultimate defeat. Hatred and conflict constitute the nature of Satan, and he uses religion to keep man separate from God. God, on the other hand, always seeks to reconcile and restore, and everything He does is motivated by love, goodwill and His desire for relationship with mankind. These are the issues with which we have to reckon when making a decision between religion and relationship with God. The choice is ours to make.

ঔ৹৵

Error and religion are always
intimidated by truth.

ঔ৹৵

Saul of Tarsus, a devout religionist, believed that he was righteous, wholeheartedly serving God through his religion, unaware that he was at variance with truth and with God. Through his experiences we see how error responds when confronted with truth. Saul of Tarsus was considered a scholar in his religion, tutored by the most prominent teachers of his time. His commitment to his religion and faith gained him respect among the religious leaders. Saul despised Jesus Christ although he had never met Him, and he was also a hater of Christ's followers. One of Jesus' followers, Stephen, a young man full of faith and power, had been working great miracles among the people and many, including several priests, had been converted to the faith. As a result, Stephen was brought before the religious council. As Saul and his associates in religion listened to Stephen expound the scriptures and prove Jesus Christ as the Jewish Messiah, they were "cut to the heart" and wanted Stephen dead and out of the way (Acts 7).

Stephen's knowledge of the first covenant scriptures, coupled with the doctrine of Jesus Christ, was a threat to their religion and the position of influence they held. Truth and error had collided. Saul and his colleagues concluded that Stephen should be silenced by stoning. They determined to send a strong message to the other followers of Jesus Christ. The killing of Stephen was a warning to them that they would suffer the same fate if they continued to preach the doctrine of Jesus Christ. Error and religion are always intimidated by truth, and react aggressively.

In the course of stoning Stephen to death, Saul and his colleagues received a convincing witness of the power of Stephen's Christianity and of his relationship with Jesus Christ, God the Father, and the Holy Spirit. Stephen's last words were his prayer to God and Jesus Christ, asking Them to forgive his executioners of their sins of religious hatred and murder. This was to his executioners, a convincing testimony of the power of Christianity over religion—truth over error, love over hate. It served to prepare Saul for his encounter with the risen and glorified Christ some days later.

Religion crumbles in the
presence of Truth.

Saul's meeting with Jesus Christ was dramatic, powerful, and compelling. Jesus intercepted Saul while he was on his way to Damascus with a letter from the Chief Priest which granted him permission to arrest and imprison all the Christians in that city. Jesus greeted Saul with a mere taste of His presence which was so overpowering that it knocked him off his horse and took away his sight. Immediately, Saul realized that what the Christians believed and preached was indeed true—Jesus Christ is risen from the dead and is the Messiah and Savior of the world. Saul's religion crumbled in the presence of Truth—Jesus Christ. Saul had no viable religious argument to present in his defense. His only response was to acknowledge Jesus as Lord and to inquire, "Lord, what wilt thou have me to do?" In the face of Truth, he came to the realization that he was a sinner, that Jesus Christ was the only One who could redeem man's sins and that, in spite of his religious zeal, he was in need of salvation.

> *And I thank Christ Jesus our Lord, who hath enabled me, for that he counted me faithful, putting me into the ministry; [13]Who was before a blasphemer, and a persecutor, and injurious: but I obtained mercy, because I did it ignorantly in unbelief.[14]And the grace of our Lord was exceeding abundant with faith and love which is in Christ Jesus.[15]This is a faithful saying, and*

worthy of all acceptation, that Christ Jesus came into the world to save sinners; of whom I am chief.

—1 Timothy 1:12–15

No good works, no chanting or burning of anything, no amount of religious practices could have brought about Saul's heart change; only an encounter with Jesus Christ . . . an encounter with Truth Himself.

In one moment, this religious tyrant, who had been so enraged at the thought of Christ and His followers converting Jews to Christianity, gave up his own religion and became a "Christ-ian" (Christian). Saul, upon reaching his destination, started to preach to the Jews there, that Christ is the Messiah and Savior of the world. Saul, having himself experienced the difference between religion and relationship with the risen Christ, now had a clearer understanding of Stephen's Christianity. Now aware of the fallacy of his self-righteousness and the vanity of his religious practices, he realized that Stephen's love, faith, and obedience to Jesus Christ, even in the face of persecution, was indeed true righteousness.

When the Chief Priest and religious elders heard that Saul was now a Christian, and that he went about pleading with the Jews to accept Jesus Christ as Messiah, they ordered Saul's death. Just a few days ago, Saul was their champion. Now he was their enemy.

The collision between Christianity and religion has not ended. It continues every day all over the world. We see clearly that Christianity and religion are opposites.

Christianity will ultimately triumph because one day Christ will confront the world and everyone will confess that Jesus Christ is Savior and Lord, as Saul did (Philippians 2:10–11).

It is my hope that you too, like Saul, when confronted with truth, would move from religion to relationship—repent of your sins, give your heart to Jesus Christ and be saved.

Chapter 12

Religion vs. Christianity

❧❧

Religion is man trying to find God...
Christianity is God finding man—
through Jesus Christ.

❧❧

It has been conclusively proven throughout this book that God and religion are not the same, and that, whereas God desires communion with man which leads to righteousness, religion denies man this nearness to God and only leads to misplaced righteousness.

Some believe and teach that Christ's Christianity and "Christian religion" are one and the same. They are not! Christ's Christianity is God-ordained while "Christian religion" is man-made. One is diametrically opposed to the other.

Religion is man trying to find God, to appease Him through religious acts in order to obtain forgiveness for his sins. Christianity is God finding man through Jesus Christ, Whose blood was shed for the remission of sins.

This is the plain and simple teaching of the Word of God. Christ's Christianity and "Christian religion" are as far apart as the east is from the west.

☙❧

No one can have a relationship with God without Jesus Christ.

☙❧

Further, Christianity is the reuniting of man with God, for man was separated from God due to sin. Through the sacrifice of Christ as the penalty for man's sins, Jesus Christ became the only mediator between God and man.

> *Neither is there salvation in any other: for there is none other name under heaven given among men, whereby we must be saved.*
> —*Acts 4:12*

Religion, with its forms, rituals, traditions, and practices, has no place in Christ's atonement for man's sins; neither can it reunite man with God, as many have been taught and are being taught. The adhering to a prescribed religious order which has been ordained by man is not supported in the Word of God. The Apostle Paul rebuked the church at Galatia for having embraced "another gospel"—one other than the Christianity that

Jesus Christ instituted which had brought them into salvation and personal relationship with the Trinity. This is the gospel that they had originally received from Paul, and from which they had deviated.

> *I marvel that ye are so soon removed from him that called you into the grace of Christ unto another gospel:[7] Which is not another; but there be some that trouble you, and would pervert the gospel of Christ.[8] But though we, or an angel from heaven, preach any other gospel unto you than that which we have preached unto you, let him be accursed.[9] As we said before, so say I now again, if any man preach any other gospel unto you than that ye have received, let him be accursed.[10] For do I now persuade men, or God? or do I seek to please men? for if I yet pleased men, I should not be the servant of Christ.*
> —Galatians 1:6–10

Early in God's relationship with man, God said that man shall not live by bread alone, but by every word that proceeds from the mouth of God.

> *All the commandments which I command thee this day shall ye observe to do, that ye may live, and multiply, and go in and possess the land which the LORD sware unto your fathers. [2]And thou shalt remember all the way which the LORD thy God led*

thee these forty years in the wilderness, to humble thee, and to prove thee, to know what was in thine heart, whether thou wouldest keep his commandments, or no. ³And he humbled thee, and suffered thee to hunger, and fed thee with manna, which thou knewest not, neither did thy fathers know; that he might make thee know that man doth not live by bread only, but by every word that proceedeth out of the mouth of the LORD doth man live.

—Deuteronomy 8:1–3

When we leave the Word of God out of our lives, we leave God out of our lives. Furthermore, no one can have a relationship with God without Jesus Christ—the only intermediary between God and man—and without adherence to the Word of God. To think otherwise is misplaced thinking.

Religion promises man what it does not have to give and what it does not have the power to perform.

Religion has not, does not, and cannot serve the purposes of God in man's life, that is, to remove sin, and to restore relationship and fellowship with God. If it did, and if it could, the state of man's heart should have been different by this time. Jesus Christ is the only One who could deliver man from sin and transform his heart to believe and to live as God intends. It was for this very purpose that He came. Religion promises man what it does not have to give and what it does not have the power to perform. Religion offers a hope that is never realized, and eventually leaves its followers empty and disappointed, hopeless and desperate, and this is sometimes dangerous. The hope that man needs can only come through a personal relationship with God through Jesus Christ.

Religion has served to drive man further away from God.

Religion has become the most powerful entity in the world because, like a virtual placebo, it tricks the individual into a belief and an acceptance of well-being, right-standing, and satisfaction. There is no truth, or experience to validate religion's claim that it can give man salvation. None whatsoever! On the contrary, with all its pomp and religiosity, religion has not been able to make man or the world better. Rather, it has served to drive man further away from God. When we put our faith and trust in something that fails to help us in time of need, we eventually turn away from it in search of something else. If that "something else" is not able to meet our needs, we try another. When everything we have tried fails, we give up on believing in God altogether, and we then accuse Him of having failed us. The truth is, God has not failed us; we have failed ourselves by believing in doctrines and rituals that are untrue rather than in God, who alone is Truth, who gave us life, whose air we breathe to live, and who gives us a brain and intelligence to think and to respond to the God-consciousness He has placed within us.

God has made man with a free will to choose. If we choose to allow man and his religion to make us puppets, mindlessly following meaningless forms and rituals, and then accuse God when we fail, we demonstrate unjust thinking. On the other hand, many can testify that when their religious beliefs had failed them and they turned to Jesus Christ, they found what they had been hoping to find in their religion, but did not.

If I am to come even close to achieving the purpose of this book, which is to recover the truth about righteousness, I must not delay in urging you to believe the reports on the ravages of religion that manifest themselves in so many different ways—wars, poverty, murders, bondages, brain washings and more. If you choose not to believe what you see and hear regarding these acts of religion, then you have already chosen religion instead of God and ultimately, you have chosen eternal separation from God.

These statements are not a matter of my personal opinion. They are a matter of fact, and the evidence is there for all to clearly see. Is God in religion that promotes the slaughter of the innocent ones who do not believe in their religion? Does God inspire men to spawn every form of evil under the banner of religion, and then politicize it to get men to believe that their brand of religion is truth? Does God create in man this pathogenic thirst for power to control other men? Would God endorse such control which would deny men the opportunity to respond to the God-consciousness in them—that God-consciousness which God has placed in the heart of every man to know God personally through the working of His Spirit, the Holy Spirit?

Religion has created more disputes, more wars and taken more lives than any other conflict known to man. God is not the author of conflict among His creation. God is Love and love does not incite wars, hatred, and brutality. Love does not enslave men to serve their masters so their masters could rise to power, fame, and riches, while the enslaved die and enter eternity separated from God. Love is not in the capture and enslavement of man's will so that man may live contrary to God's will and God's laws. Religion does this! These evils are there for the world to see, but the world is not seeing because religion has done a good job of blinding the hearts and clouding the intelligence of those who subscribe to it, whether by choice, by deception or by force.

The spirit of religion is so powerful that, although devotees have become disenchanted because God did not show up, they remain loyal and still maintain a religious façade. The Spirit of God, who was sought in the time of need, was decidedly absent, and so they no longer look to that religion to find God, yet amazingly, their devotion remains. To expect to find God in such places is misplaced expectation. It is the Spirit of God who gives life, and when God is absent there is no spiritual life to be gained.

> *It is the spirit that quickeneth; the flesh profiteth nothing: the words that I speak unto you, they are spirit, and they are life.*
>
> —*John 6:63*

Many church edifices therefore, are now merely museums which draw a continuous flow of tourists who are sympathizers of the particular religion.

To some, Christianity is identified by an outward sign or symbol. To others, Christianity is characterized by prescribed religious observances which are intended to show men's piety to God and through which they claim to have their sins forgiven. Jesus Christ did not instruct His disciples to wear outward symbols to identify themselves as Christians or as a sign of being righteous. One might wear symbols to identify himself as a believer but the wearing of symbols does not make him a believer. The disciples had something far greater, which also spoke much louder. It was their relationship with Jesus Christ, with God the Father, and with one another. Jesus had taught them that the world would know them by their love one to another, not by religious symbols. This is how the Christians lived and this is how they were identified as Christians. When people saw how they interacted with one another, demonstrating Christ's love, they knew they belonged to Jesus Christ and referred to them as "Christ-ians." It is out of this God-ordained relationship among the "Christ-ians," that the name *Christian* emerged.

> *And when he had found him, he brought him unto Antioch. And it came to pass, that a whole year they assembled themselves with the church, and taught much people. And the disciples were called Christians first in Antioch:*
>
> —*Acts 11:26*

These Christians became "The Church." They had no buildings. They had Christ and each other. The emphasis in Christianity was and will always be relationship with Jesus Christ, the Father, the Holy Spirit, and with each other. Nothing else and no other way could be justifiably termed Christian.

The Church was one body of believers, and still is. That "body" is one unit and can never be disjointed or splintered.

There is one body, and one Spirit, even as ye are called in one hope of your calling; ⁵ One Lord, one faith, one baptism,

—*Ephesians 4:4–5*

The Church may spread out to different locations but it still is the Church, singular. Jesus Christ is the one who referred to His followers as the Church. He is the Head of the Church and Savior of His body of believers.

For the husband is the head of the wife, even as Christ is the head of the church: and he is the saviour of the body.

—*Ephesians 5:23*

The early Christians understood this and united in love within this Christ-ordained structure, and the Church flourished in the power of the Holy Spirit.

Chapter 13

The Holy Spirit's Role in Propagating Truth

❧❧

To become the Church that God
intended us to be, we must return to
Biblical Christianity.

❧❧

The Church today is far removed from the Church
that Jesus Christ instituted, chiefly because deviations, distortions, and misrepresentations of the gospel
have been embraced and proliferated as truth. The
early Church was a powerful, dynamic organism. They
impacted the known world, propagating the gospel of
Jesus Christ and making disciples of men, as Jesus had
commissioned, although they faced untold opposition
and persecution. This was possible for them, because in
the face of all odds, they practiced Biblical Christianity.
They held fast to God's truth and to His prescribed methods of propagating that truth. If we are to become the

Church that God intended us to be, we must return to Biblical Christianity. We must re-examine what constitutes God's truth and embrace, once again, His ordained method of propagating that truth.

After Jesus Christ had accomplished His mission on earth and gone back to Heaven, He did not leave His followers to just "do the best they could" in carrying out His ministry. Jesus was not unaware of their limitations to accomplish the task. To ensure that the gospel of Jesus Christ would stay on the course that Jesus had established, He sent the Holy Spirit, as promised, to dwell in the hearts of His disciples, and in the heart of every believer who would prove their love for Him.

> *Howbeit when he, the Spirit of truth, is come, he will guide you into all truth: for he shall not speak of himself; but whatsoever he shall hear, that shall he speak: and he will shew you things to come.*
>
> *—John 16:13*

The Holy Spirit had come on the Day of Pentecost and had indeed proven to be that enabling power they had needed to carry on in the absence of Jesus Christ, and so the early Church thrived. These early believers clung steadfastly to the Word of God, and the Spirit of God worked with them and led them by way of truth, reminding them of all that Jesus had taught. It was the Holy Spirit who had inspired them to be "Truth-Bearers" rather than "Opinion-Bearers" or religious propagators and practitioners.

The early Church never deviated from Jesus' vision and mission, or from His teachings and methods. Relying completely on the leading of the Holy Spirit, they propagated the gospel of Jesus Christ without compromise. As a result, miraculous signs and wonders followed, and many were added to the Church daily. The disciples knew that the Holy Spirit was the key to the advancement of the Church and Christianity. They knew that without Him they would fail.

As much as a natural man needs the air he breathes to sustain his natural life, we need the Holy Spirit to live this Christian life.

God has not changed His methods. We cannot effectively represent Jesus Christ and His Word without the participation of the Holy Spirit. He is our Teacher, our Guide, our Strength, and our Revelator. He is the One through Whose influence the officers appointed by Jesus Christ are able to bring clarity to the Word of God. As much as a natural man needs the air he breathes to sustain his natural life, we need the Holy Spirit to live this Christian life. It is He who enables those of the Christian faith to live by the Word of God for effective Christian living.

∂∘∘⊛

Because the Holy Spirit has not been allowed His rightful place, the Church today has lost its influence and power.

∂∘∘⊛

Today, however, many Church leaders are trying to represent Jesus Christ without the Holy Spirit. They have replaced the Holy Spirit and the Word of God with religious programs, and legalistic rules and regulations, none of which Jesus Christ appointed. It is precisely because the Holy Spirit has not been allowed His rightful place in the advancing of the Church of Jesus Christ, that the Church today has lost its influence and power. Where are the supernatural signs, wonders, healings, miracles, and the convicting and sustaining power that once gave proof of the gospel of Jesus Christ?

True godly leadership in the Church of Jesus Christ allows the Holy Spirit to inspire, guide, and influence the direction of the Church. It is important that every Christian should make the clear distinction between natural leadership and the leadership of the Holy Spirit. The Holy Spirit knows the mind of God and leads us according to the will of God. Unless this distinction is made, the "**un**-holy" spirit could influence believers to follow a path of error and cause confusion which would affect their thinking, believing, and way of living. When the Holy Spirit is not allowed to lead, the believers could easily embrace man-made rituals and programs.

We must take into consideration that some people are born with natural leadership qualities and abilities. This is a natural gift from God for the purpose of providing good secular leadership. Such persons possess charisma that causes people to look up to them and follow them. Natural leadership could be developed and enhanced through institutions of learning, and by experience.

Good, godly leadership, on the other hand, is never attained by natural learning. The purpose of spiritual leadership is to build and equip the Body of Christ which is a spiritual organism that finds its life through the work of the Spirit. It must therefore be sustained by spiritual means. Spiritual leadership can only be received as a spiritual gift from Jesus Christ and the Father, and administered through the Holy Spirit. When this occurs, natural leadership skills, combined with this spiritual gift of leadership, can give the individual added advantages.

Furthermore, Jesus Christ has entrusted spiritual gifts to men to benefit the Church and to convince the world of the reality of the gospel of Jesus Christ. These gifts transform ordinary men into extraordinary men, making them prominent spiritual leaders in their particular sphere of ministry. It is only with complete reliance on the Holy Spirit and absolute adherence to the truth of God's Word that church leaders and Christians could effectively administer the gospel of Jesus Christ and continue to build Christ's Church, against which the gates of hell would not be able to prevail.

Where is the Holy Spirit in most of the Christian Church today? If He is not there, where has He gone, and why has He gone? These questions should not be ignored. To do so would result in even more pervasive lethargy, and eventual paralysis. We must find the answers and do what is required to have the Holy Spirit again residing in the hearts of believers and in the Church. The solution is not in more fasting, as needful as fasting is; it is not in more concerts, conferences or crusades; it is not in more street marches, with the waving of flags and banners while parading and dancing in the streets to the musical beat of the world. These efforts will not secure the return of the Holy Spirit. God has offered His own solution:

> *If my people, which are called by my name, shall humble themselves and pray, and seek my face, and turn from their wicked ways; then will I hear from heaven, and will forgive their sin, and will heal their land.*
> *—2 Chronicles 7:14*

Believers must individually return to their "first love" and enter into intimate relationship with Jesus

Christ, the Holy Spirit, and the Father. Nothing else would bring the Holy Spirit back to reside in the heart of the believer and in the Church. The Word of God has not changed. God will never withhold His presence from those who earnestly seek Him with all their heart, and who are willing to return to His ways.

> *Even from the days of your fathers ye are gone away from mine ordinances, and have not kept them. Return unto me, and I will return unto you, saith the Lord of hosts.*
>
> —*Malachi 3:7a*

God continues to yearn for relationship with mankind. It is by the guidance of the Holy Spirit that His truth would be maintained and passed on from generation to generation. Any other method adopted for the propagation of the gospel will result in deviations, misrepresentations, and distortions. This would ultimately lead to misplaced righteousness.

Chapter 14

Do Not Be Deceived Any Longer

❧❧

Religion is the doorway to misplaced righteousness.

❧❧

You may recall my statement at the very start of this book that "righteousness is simply being in right standing with God." No man can be in right standing with God outside of having a personal relationship with Him. It is within this relationship with God that love, faith, and obedience are cultivated in an individual, and God alone determines when righteousness should be ascribed to that individual.

Religion, on the other hand, is the doorway to misplaced righteousness. It deceives man, causing him to rest in the fallacy that there is something in that religion that could remove his sins, and get him to God and into **His** heaven. I have established throughout these writings that no religion and no religious practice could ever take away man's sins and restore him to relationship with God. How can a religion bring you into fellowship with God when that religion teaches and practices doctrines that contradict and violate the very Word given by God to foster and preserve relationship with Him? How then could a religious man, who does not have a personal relationship with God and Jesus Christ, lead anyone to have a relationship with Him?

There is a stark difference between God's Word, and what religion teaches and practices. Examine and compare the lives of those who truly have a relationship with God and Jesus Christ, with the lives of those who believe in and follow religion, and note the vast difference. I am not talking about every one that says "God, God" or "Lord, Lord." There are a lot of those in Christian churches who simply pay nominal allegiance to Christ and are far from being doers of His Word and His will. There is counterfeit in everything and there will always be counterfeit as long as Satan—that counterfeiter and master-deceiver—is on the earth. I am talking rather, about those who live by the truth of God's Word and who demonstrate, especially in the face of difficulty, that resolute love for God, faith in God and obedience to His Word. These are the ones who God considers to be righteous.

The counterfeit attests to the fact that truth exists.

There are those who disclaim the validity and importance of God in their lives because they have seen only the counterfeit that is religion and the counterfeit and evil which exists, even within Christianity. But the counterfeit attests to the fact that truth exists. Its purpose is always to deceive and lure the unsuspecting into accepting it as that which is genuine. Do you know why there are no eleven dollar counterfeit bills? It is simply because there are no genuine eleven dollar bills in existence. You can be sure that if genuine eleven dollar bills are approved and printed by a government, eleven dollar counterfeit bills would be in circulation in that country. In the same way and for the same reason, religion is present to counterfeit the truth that is Christianity, and to derail man from having a relationship with God through Jesus Christ and from living by God's Word and His standard.

One's disbelief in the existence of God
does not make God nonexistent.

I invite you to indulge me even further as I present you with another simple analogy between God and religion, so that the utter disparity between the two becomes abundantly clear. Do you know that orange juice and orange "drink" are not the same? Orange juice is pure juice from an orange. Orange drink, on the other hand, contains part orange juice, part water, additives, and sweeteners. When the manufacturers of orange drink package it for sale, they put a picture of a delicious looking orange on the carton to give the impression that you are getting the healthy nutrients from the orange. The end result of consuming the orange juice and the orange drink is not the same. You get natural vitamin-C from the orange juice and you may well get diabetes from the orange drink. While they can both appear the same, one is life-sustaining while the other is deadly! This parallels the subtlety of religion. Be wise. Make your choice . . . orange juice or orange "drink"? . . . Jesus Christ or religion?

There are no atheists in hell. They become believers in Jesus Christ when it is too late.

Those who disclaim the validity and importance of God in their lives assume this position to be wise. This is exactly what the Counterfeiter wants. This counterfeit has been so successful that the great majority have taken the position that they would leave God out of their lives. They consider this to be intelligent and safe, but is it really? How intelligent and safe would it be when they leave this life and stand before God to answer for what they have done with the salvation that He provided for them through Jesus Christ? He is the only mediator through whom restoration of relationship with God is possible. Those who say they do not believe in "these things" must understand that one's disbelief in the existence of God does not make God nonexistent. Such thinking does not change the reality of God. Similarly, one may choose not to believe in the reality of gravity, but let him jump off a building and I guarantee you, if he survives, he would be a believer in the reality of gravity. There are no atheists in hell. They become believers in Jesus Christ when it is too late.

God did not leave man to struggle through life on his own. He provided man with His Word and His Spirit—the Spirit of Truth—to guide him into all truths through the Word of God, the Bible. God therefore, holds man responsible and accountable for his decision. God gives every man the right to choose whether he wants a relationship with Him through Jesus Christ, or not. With choices come consequences. Man is free to choose anything or anyone in place of relationship with God. Man can and does make his own god but the consequences are also his.

When the consequences of man's wrong choices face him, he often cries out, "If there is a God, where is He?" The answer is very simple. God is always present, taking note of the choices we make, and He does not interfere with the exercise of the free will He has given to us. We make the choices, not God. The consequences of our choices are ours, not God's. If you break a red light, and you are hit and killed by a car that has the green light, that driver is not guilty and is not held accountable for your death. You are. You broke the law and you face the consequence. Similarly, it would be unjust and sinful to accuse God for the consequences of the choices that we make.

When we choose religion, we, in fact, reject relationship with the Trinity and forego a life of righteousness for one lived in the deception of misplaced righteousness. Where we spend eternity would be determined by our choice.

For a person to live and die and to not know his Maker, God and Father, is life's greatest tragedy. Yet equally tragic is a life lived, presumably serving God, but actually in the deception of error. Many, though earnest and sincere, are on this broad road that leads to destruction. I urge you, dear reader . . . do not be deceived any longer!

About the Author

*A*ustin J. de Bourg is an accomplished Minister of Jesus Christ and Christian Author. His intimacy with the Trinity has gained him the privilege of receiving the revelation contained in his books, which include ***Insights into the Mystery of the Trinity, What Really is Christianity*** and ***Working the Harvest.***

Austin is a true pioneer. In 1980, he founded and began pastoring the Trinidad Christian Center, the first Independent, Full-Gospel church in that nation, which started with a revival that lasted five years, after which over 300 independent churches followed.

In his over 35 years of effective ministry, he has also established humanitarian projects in rural areas of impoverished countries where food is scarce. He has been conferred with an Honorary Doctor of Divinity Degree and is also the founder of Apostolic Revival Ministries (ARM), aimed at rekindling the apostolic spirit and ministry in the Church.

He is currently working on other book projects.

Other books by
Austin J. de Bourg:

Insights into the Mystery of the Trinity

"Why would the Almighty God need a Son and a Holy Spirit? Is He lacking in Himself? How could Jesus Christ be God and Man at the same time? Why would such a good and perfect God make such a bad devil?" These questions and more are answered in this book overflowing with revelation regarding the Trinity, Jesus Christ and Christianity. It takes the reader from eternity to Pentecost and beyond to unfold the saga of the Trinity's quest to restore man from his fallen state back into relationship, fellowship, and dialogue with God. As you read, you will discover priceless treasures that were kept secret by God . . . until now.

What Really is Christianity

This book is a wakeup call to slumbering Christians. It focuses on Christianity from God's perspective and reveals the honorable role God has ordained for Christians in His plan for mankind. It takes a look at Christianity, from an aspect rarely considered in modern times, revealing truths from the word of God on the supernatural birthright and heritage of Christians and Christianity, and answering questions on the seldom taught doctrine of the reality of man's dual nature. It deals with the misconceptions of Christianity citing the dangers of replacing 'relationship with God' with religion. It not only diagnoses the present malady of Christianity, but prescribes the corrective treatment that would bring Christians and Christianity back on the course designed by Jesus Christ.

Working the Harvest

Success, victory, and rewards await those who would bring in the harvest. This book brings the reader back in focus with the true spirit and purpose of Christianity. It highlights the biblical formula for success and reveals how to come into the hundred-fold blessings, which include divine favor, divine health, divine provision, divine protection, and freedom from satanic influences.

Author's Contact Information

Apostolic Renewal Ministries
Phone: (868) 633 1404
Email: arm@arm-tcc.org
Website: www.arm-tcc.org

Trinidad Christian Center
Phone: (868) 637 5221 or (868) 633 4037
Email: tcc@tcc1980.org
Website:www.tcc1980.org

Made in the USA
San Bernardino, CA
11 June 2016